I0750327

FINISHING LINE PRESS
www.finishinglinepress.com

EDGES OF WANTING

poems by

Judith Mary Gee

Finishing Line Press
Georgetown, Kentucky

EDGES OF WANTING

ISBN 978-1-64662-395-2 First Edition

ACKNOWLEDGMENTS

The poem "Overheard at Mongol Borei Hospital" appears in the 2019 edition of *Chautauqua.*

"Nothing So Beautiful" appears in the 2020 edition of *Chautauqua.*

"Truffe de Chine" will appear in the 2020 edition of *The New Guard.*

Publisher: Leah Huete de Maines
Editor: Christen Kincaid
Cover Art: New York Public Library
Author Photo: Judith Mary Gee
Cover Design: Elizabeth Maines McCleavy

Order online: www.finishinglinepress.com
also available on amazon.com

Author inquiries and mail orders:
Finishing Line Press
PO Box 1626
Georgetown, Kentucky 40324
USA

Table of Contents

ACCORDIONIST

Mitu was missing this morning.

Every payday I offer a dollar. So solemn,
I could be lighting a candle at Notre-Dame.

Then, like the gentleman he is, he bows before
segueing into *Waves of the Danube*
right there in the bowels of the subway.

Every other Friday, I pay for a waltz and a tango.
Every other Wednesday, you're wired for chemo.

At a sweatshop for intellectuals, I make
the cogs mesh, whistle, and hum. Days open and close,
notes high and low, keyboard partnering bellows.

Everything's gone up. Costs an arm and a leg.
Then, *sotto voce,* you explain
you're in Stage 4, buying time.

Every other Friday, I'll pay for a waltz and a tango.
Every other Wednesday, you were wired for chemo.

AERIALIST

Along the midway and underneath the arcade,
the smell and feel of the carnival
slapped up against the crowds.

We'd hit these hick towns—whistle stops
where the world is small. The locals came
with their loose change.

They'd line up to see a flash of flesh—
a golden girl, a gaudy girl.
I'd be in razzle-dazzle red.
I'd stop traffic.

The marks all thought they owned me.
They'd be watching
with those silver-round eyes.

I used to think,
They got the money to make me.

I knew they loved the mutants
more than me. I'd always
have to work twice as hard
to get half as much attention.

It never felt right in my gut.
I knew it was time to shift gears.

I got my act together.

No more wolf whistles
and octopus arms for me!
I had a hunger
for the high wire.

I strutted my stuff.
Four complete revolutions
in midair.

No one could touch me.

I received a standing ovation.
But you got to do it twice
for them to really believe you.
You got to do it *bigger*.
I'm a pretty hard act
for myself to follow.

So this is what they call
"show business." One minute
they're throwing roses.
The next, tomatoes.

I said to myself, *Do I dare?*
I dared.
I was working without a net.

I saw my shadow twisting, falling.
The shadow collected light and air.
Now I was what
I never wanted to be. Helpless.

The words came from my mouth.
"I'm hurt, I'm hurt."

The crowd came closer.
They wanted to see the pretty girl cry.

In the air was the only place
I ever felt really comfortable.
I thought I could do anything.
I grabbed at stars.

Lying here like this, I can't help
feeling this carny life
has left me high and dry.

AFTERWARD

One leg up, she washes herself
under her tail. That salmon tongue,
abrasive and efficient, runs
its warm length over her privates.
Self-aware, un-self-conscious,
she takes her bath, giving herself
prickly kisses. I know that touch
better than yours.

Amber eyes narrow into slits
of perception. Her squint finds me;
the head moves slightly. Old Mama Cat—
she still knows me. Years ago,
I watched her only litter
emerge: mouth, mouth,
mouth, mouth, mouth. Now,
haughty as ever, she pauses
to inspect me. Her sensitive nose
registers the unfamiliar. Murmuring to herself,
she rubs her face over my clothes,
smelling your sweat.

ANGEL CRIES AT MIDNIGHT

Even now from my stony perch
close to where they think it's heaven
their thoughts overlap like bed linen
my motto might be look don't touch
I hold my wings close to my sides
so tired of this perfection
always knowing never having
the luxury of doubt
unable to look into someone else's eyes
to see my real face reflected twice
    A cup of coffee
    please
    and if you can spare it
    a kiss

Is it true that hot air rises
far from the glitter and the grit
no one worries about a lack of heat
and hot water is merely a concept
in the land of the absolute
colors have no meaning
days when the air hung clear
I never wanted a thing
now for the first time
every desire comes to me
    A cup of coffee
    please
    and if you can spare it
    a kiss

I watch their thin shadows
each cool as a death and separate
pressed against the thick wall
they undulate like flames
hell I have seen it in my solitude
I am no longer complacent
I want to muddy my shoes where they do
to sweat to eat bread
to be slapped by the wind
to enter the city of dreamers and live
    A cup of coffee
    please
    and if you can spare it
    a kiss

BECAUSE THE HORIZON WAS ALWAYS

so far, we raced after it, hellbent
on dancing uptown at the Apollo before turning
twenty-one, sure such a feat

would change everything. The same untruth
repeated about sending ordinary men into space.

Monitoring what they saw as
a miracle, the rest of the world continued
holding its breath. They were all touching down
together in one of the flat lunar maria,

the Sea of Tranquility. *I did not see it,*
so I did not believe it.

Fifty years after the *Eagle,* out of breath
and time, your body is on view;
your voice, on mixtape: "Amazing Grace." "Ave Maria."

BED

I'm off the grid when I climb in: Enormous
to myself, I pledge my body to the queen, though
others judge me fit only for the single.

My iron ship, curlicued to the hilt, lined with
a mattress the manufacturer has named Cannes,
guarantees a roundtrip to unspeakable dreamland,

but every time I surrender my vision, unfiltered
information becomes a montage of memory:

Rising oceans comprise the problem of the century.

Economists refer to these past ten years as a lost decade.

Without benefit of a shark cage, a sixty-four-year-old woman
is now swimming from Cuba to Florida.

Light rain, filigree on the window, tapped
like fingers when I last shut down.

CHARLES BRIDGE

The old actor is crossing
now, in search of food
as well as light. Alongside
him on the egg-fortified
cobblestones chug the still
photographer and the dialogue
coach, spitting out
the unholy trinity: salt, fat, and
carbohydrates. Suddenly pellets
of real hail are dappling down
the storied cheekbones. He has squandered
the shank of this weekend saving himself
for his big death scene.

Monday morning at Barrandov
Studios, his young costar
will bash him on the head
with a sword; two crew members
will trip over wires; and
his nineteenth-century
costume will come undone while
the cameras are rolling. Braziers
will render the set even hotter,
and falling plastic snow
will get stuck in his wig. Worse,
he will shake a fistful
of unscripted tears.

But the skyline tonight
is marzipan as he smiles and half-
listens to his comrades proposing
a side trip to Budapest. Soon there
will be a round table beneath
a chandelier (each bulb embraced
by a pair of white wings). And
he has even left behind at the hotel
the plastic bottle of martinis. For
tonight the grimy statue being rubbed
for luck shakes its martyr head and
the dingy halo of stars. All week long,
this stranger in tinted lenses has been
stealing the sun in Bohemia. Who knows
what local treasures these countless
peddlers are offering? Who sees the faces
of those kneeling beggars? All eyes focus
in one direction whenever
the old actor is crossing.

CODA

Like an uptown whore, my daughter
makes her big mouth a bright red gash.
My southern thrush has painted eyebrows,
and I do not mind listening to its jargon.
Better geese than girls! (Better bird than bitch!)

The days my solitude refused to feed me,
I would beat my child with cheap
wooden chopsticks till she uttered a sound
like the end of the world. I wanted her
to help mind the store; she danced away
in black fishnet stockings.

I do not smoke. I do not drink.
I do not play mah-jongg to earn
my passage through the dark.
With my little Warrior, I have
roots and wings, everything but time.

I walk among olive kin
the shape of bells, paler
than a monk's robe.
Forsythia. Four whispering syllables
I once could not pronounce
(so like names and faces from my past
it would be indiscreet to mention).

I hear colors from my *hua mei*'s throat;
cinnabar and jade echo throughout
our humble neighborhood park.
Yet I know it is singing by rote,
set in its ways

like an old man.

COMMUTE
(IN HELL, IT'S ALWAYS MONDAY MORNING)

How I've witnessed Joe Buddha on the Culver local. That's F
to you, buddy. His baseball cap catches my eye

NIRVANA

but then I'm thrown by the back of his denim jacket

SIN CITY

Jupiter just got bopped by a rock! he announces

and chants *Bebop, bibimbap, bebop, bibimbap, bebop, bibimbap.*

As we're being held at the station
momentarily by the omnipotent
train dispatcher, Joe Buddha explains

the vast loneliness of cities
is just another form of river blindness.

Departing the car, I overhear Joe
Buddha requesting of the other passengers

a few coins to ease the remainder
of this blessed journey, some smiles, or a spare

apple? sandwich? can of soda?
as a testament to the glory.

Underground still, I haul myself
up those stairs lured by melancholy
solo violin offered by a Slav in light blue

long an Internet sensation but still underground;
he deserves Carnegie as I,

one red velvet seat.

COOKING

Hair slicked down extra, the maître d'
bribed and swore to secrecy
busboys and waiters,
leaving to their discretion
the House of Exquisite Taste

while he slithered away
to the Center of the Universe
so he could worship Duke Ellington.

After the show came the showdown.
An umbrella smacked his back;

spokes splintered and fabric tattered.

Then said umbrella thudded to the floor, a carcass
transmogrifying: Peking duck for those
who wouldn't know the difference
between opium and monosodium glutamate.

But so what? Sure as anything, he'd visited Heaven,
grooving to such as that "Creole Love Call"
like anybody else who could buck and wing.

GARDENIA IN THE RAIN

A voice whose owner had heard the rain
and thunder of applause was once here,
in need of violins and chow mein.

Jonesing like hell, she did not complain;
beyond the Foo dogs and boutonniere,
a voice whose owner had heard the rain

and the uncorking of good Champagne
would not be served by a cavalier
in need of violins and chow mein.

Monkey rode her back, drove her insane,
pulled the sweet flower above her ear.
A voice whose owner had heard the rain

sang of devils she could not explain
to uniformed flunkies who stood there
in need of violins and chow mein.

No high yaller stud without a brain,
no priest, no police can commandeer
a voice whose owner had heard the rain,
in need of violins and chow mein.

THE GINKGO HUNTERS OF CENTRAL PARK

With so many other edibles (high bush
cranberries, sassafras roots ...) available,
who in the world
would go near those fetid trees?

They are all elderly, all Asian,
park officials claim, *and all delighted*
to be there on hands and knees.

Some arrive with shopping carts
to collect their treasure: the stinko ginkgo.
From early autumn into December,
their gnarly fingers sift through
leaves like tiny gold fans
no eyes can hide behind. Their gnarly fingers

squeeze the berries no one else
will go near. The air takes on that
awful smell, natural but inhuman;
and a ginkgo nut emerges, tender and desired.

With so many other edibles (chicory,
mugwort, lady's thumb ...) available,
who in his right mind
would come near these fetid trees?

They are all Asian, all elderly,
park officials repeat, *and all*
their grandchildren get into MIT.

KARAOKE AT THE OLD FOLKS HOME

Smugly self-righteous, these numbers
roll out of mouths even when
no one is watching the screen up front.

Mostly military or religious, songs this
uncompromising get on my nerves.

Some of our pals from the dementia ward
seem to keep tune the best.

The general and the hunchback detective
refuse to participate. They're widowers
and gossip like you wouldn't believe.

I'm next to my old man. We both wear
horizontal stripes and wire-rimmed glasses.
(If he turns and sees my eyes, I'll just
say I've got hay fever or conjunctivitis.)

He maneuvers his cane pretty well, tapping
the gray-green carpet, or
threatening the occasional troublemaker.

I like to imagine he can recall
the likes of Billie Holiday or Artie Shaw.

Maybe, because of the preponderance
of women, he smiles because he thinks
this is a whorehouse.

My old man is getting well. Nothing less
could be possible. And just around the corner,
maybe next week, everyone in this room

will be spared. Till then, hallelujah, Buddha,
we fight on.

LANDING

"Oh, no, it wasn't the airplanes. It was Beauty killed the Beast."
—Soundtrack of King Kong *(1933)*

Come here, you big hairy man,
and show me your chest.
I want to see what kind of pillow
it will make. So open your shirt
and let me in where it's warm.
I'd like to traverse your
whole huge body. Let me climb
up your knees as though they were
cliffs. I want to sit
right in your navel. Your mother
would want it that way, a nice girl
like me nestling where the cord
was connected. So be a good boy
and make way for the champ—the ace
of them all, best lady pilot
you'll ever meet. We'll have
a smooth flight. I'll rev up
my little engine and nosedive
into your heart. You set my tail spinning.
You know I like a furry face. Honey,
every whisker is a charm. I think
you'll like me, too. Want proof?
Just as Fay Wray undid that ape,
so I'll undo you.

MERCY

The tyrannical oak inclined to kill
grants a reprieve. The man emerges from the annex
to brush snow off the deck. His hands no longer

fists, the knuckles are now relaxed, if red. He watches
for the moon to graft onto a branch
so he will have something new to offer: *moonfruit.*

He can still taste the hard cider she snatched
from the tabernacle of commerce
where they praised her dancing

but paid little. He will always hear
her cantabile chatter. *Got a bandage?*
I am bleeding. I am broken.

Each snowflake, masquerading as a star,
conspires with the tree. A branch eight inches in diameter
is penetrating the roof of the main house. *Got a bottle?*

I am bluestocking. I am bitter. Each star
distorts and distracts. He loses sight of the oak there, waiting.
Got a bed? I am bereft. I am bare.

MOTHER IN MYANMAR

Johnny and Luther sprang from my loins
like babes of wild Indochinese tigers
my husband drinks but manages to steal a few chickens
the rivers tell stories we hand down to survive
so we continue our green country changes names
I have no tea no sweet dumplings no lipstick
but I have twins and their tongues are black and holy

Johnny and Luther sprang from my arms
to lead our people against the evil Yangon
no looting no cursing this is God's Army
a candle to hold a tree to sit under
a hymn that praises the good fight
I have no news but I hear they look different
Luther's head is partly shaved Johnny looks like a girl

Johnny and Luther sprang from my heart
out into the wilderness to the borderline
finally surrendering with a fistful of disciples
to the new kings of Siam or Thailand or Hell
M16 assault rifles cheroots Bibles
I have no hope in this forest of rain
trees like child soldiers fall down

You who believe in Christ the Redeemer
you who believe in the Buddha of Compassion
may you find your way over the mountain
to a peace I will never know

NOTHING SO BEAUTIFUL

as a nitrate print appears on the black ice
this evening. Neither Garbo nor Gish vehicle unspools
across the concrete. Only the half-blind émigré and I
present ourselves to the boulevard. In the gutter reclines snow,
a drunken coven we harass repeatedly with our boots
as if chasing ghosts. The half-blind émigré, hooded against fate,

reminisces about Odessa and her former occupation, engineer
of *automaticity*. I listen like a thief in training, noting
just how many turns will yield her cache of memories.
But nothing so beautiful as a nitrate print
emerges from her tales of wild dogs, subsidized housing,
and queuing up for rations. And the half-blind émigré,

needing more than I have left, demands to know, *If I fall,*
will you be there? In the gutter recedes snow,
a nitrate river devoid of bodies. I refuse
to read aloud those intertitles. She insists
The Little Tramp was nothing but a pervert.
So we move on, co-conspirators no more. Black ice awaits.

OVERHEARD AT MONGOL BOREI HOSPITAL

It was listening for my footsteps
as I gathered firewood. Just as on
any given day. Maybe I stepped an inch
or two this way or that, counting
the blessings of heaven. *I have no lice.*
Now I know: Some truths defy imagining.

Really, I was out there for just
rice money. People with a truck used to
buy the wood. My regular customers.
I have no pockmarks. Then I heard it
explode with that malicious laugh: one more
land mine, gut straight out of Motorola.

Hard to detect, harder to defang.
Bandits spending every path in their way
like stolen money. Pockets emptied of regret.
I have no venereal disease.
The glare of metal makes me flinch.
For sixty cents, I have lost my leg
and any chance for marriage.

PRACTICE

When I pucker my mouth
and send through breath,
I can make sound, but no song.

It seems to elude me,
this secret of music.
The inner edges of lips meet
and they are the edges of wanting.
Hunger. You hear breathiness,
urgency, anxiety. Corners are pushed
forward. Reaching. The smile is lost.

Speaking. I am of no use
to myself. Small persistent noises.
Trying to make the sound whole.
Holding together. Lips. Speaking in
whispers. Persuasion. *Yes. Please.*
Drawing through breath. Roundness.
I want to. Wetness.
And again.
Pushing. And again.

I have entered
the domain of birds.
Listen to me.
Whistling.

RECONNAISSANCE

Circumventing the leap
from frying pan to fire,

I employ peripheral vision
to verify which one might be after me.

The devil I know curls its tail
even when that is out of fashion.
The devil I do not know advocates
extreme straight-razor shaving.

Circumventing the leap
from frying pan to fire,

I lift my crumpled-tissue skirts
to verify which one might be after me.

The devil I know strokes too soft, slams too hard,
does not possess a fine-gauge filter for untidy emotions.
The devil I do not know remains impassive as a clock.

Circumventing the leap
from frying pan to fire,

I pivot one hundred and eighty degrees
to verify which one might be after me.

The devil I know undergoes fermentation.
The devil I do not know refuses to biodegrade.

REVISITING SWANS

The S neck straightens. Sleevelike
wings flail and turn into
the articulate arms of this
faux virgin. I am never lonely
in a red velvet chair: Another curtain
hunches its multiple shoulders
and my real life, along with the dusk,

begins like a first flutter.
I watch and learn that love exists
only to make us sweat and pray.
Fasting girls in the corps prepare
to smudge their toe shoes once again
on a lake the color of repentance.
Their feet blister and bleed.

In the moonlight, Siegfried is demanding
the truth. "Mama's tears fill this lake,"
mimes Odette, a mute swan. In the spotlight:
a *pas de deux*. Then she glimpses
his birthday crossbow, discarded but
still lethal. "Hunter!" she hisses.
I am sure I saw pale eyelids

flutter that July evening. I know
she was spelling my full name
for the wedge of nuns; each letter
rippling through her consciousness
sur les pointes before obliging
the lake where her own daughter
would be turned into a swan.

SCRIMSHAW

A cage of bone,
a cage of flesh—that's what
it was to me. When I cursed
God to His face, that's when they knew
I was leaving. I have been
on the sea some years now.
And I do not regret leaving home.
I have learned to live this life.
I have learned it to my marrow.

I have learned to carve
pictures others prize. I have taken
baleen straight from the beast
and held it up against the sun.
The light to see images. Ships
I have dreamed nights on the water,
ships I have seen up close.

I have held my knife
to the jaw, changed it
from its natural state. And
this betrayal
glares at me from the side
of the blade. My design is borne on
this piece of work, color of
some woman's skin.

SLEEP

Once you slept with one eye open,
ready to fend off the demons of hunger
with a clenched fist or a heart so full
of dreaming, it made the stomach shrink
with shame. In those days the night
held only the ominous buzzing
of a thousand restless insects,
the rustling of sheets
patched more than once, or else
the thunder and lightning
of a sudden storm.

Perhaps if we had slept that way,
with one eye open (at least in winter,
at least in summer), we might
have seen it coming, caught on
to your tricks a bit sooner.
The gradual loss of memory,
and the shaking, and the falls.
But your voice remained the same,
high-pitched, almost singing,
aphoristic. *Always prepare for flight.*
For what good is hindsight?

Somewhere in the voiceless air,
there is the sound of your breathing,
so shallow it would not fill
the cup of anyone human, so
you are no longer human.
If it must be, we once said,
so be it. Our eyelids slid down,
heavy as rain-soaked clothes,
or rotted wooden boats filled
to the brim with memories
and ghosts. We exhaled
carelessly, as though breath
would always be abundant.
So be it, you nodded
in the strange white room, closing
the door in our faces and

both of your eyes.

TIME, A THIEF

Robbed of your childhood, you slowly
took on the appearance of a thief,
slinking against walls, hiding in corners,
inhabiting shadows. You became
a shadow in a furnished room, your bed
shrouded in smoke that was sweet-smelling,
contraband. You entered the fillings
in someone else's mouth just to catch
the random radio signals: the music, the news.

You sailed your bicycle through the somewhat
magical night, suddenly a kid again
by way of tablet or capsule, going, going,
lost but loving it completely, stopping up
the crevices of your life with something
unreal, getting stuck in time
as though it were tar, baby, and you
the proud wearer of feathers, at once
special and just another acid queen, dragging.

Robbed of old age, you have become a thief,
flickering in and out of hallways,
a phantom lightbulb, sallow and bald
before burning out. You go out
to the dancehall of the damned, where
they compare scars like fashion accessories
and sing the same old songs of parents
missing in action, dreams that short-circuited,
loves snatched up like cigarette butts.
You never wanted to turn forty.
Now you may get your wish.

TRIPTYCH

A map of everywhere he has flown
and everyone he has not found, his face
brushes hers. On the coldest V-Day
in the city's history, he is pleading
his case to a worshiper of animals
who shuns the number four. In his
seventies, he now pledges to follow
flight patterns of birds instead of planes.

Friendly and enemy radars continued to detect
a surfeit of information; a deficit
of knowledge. *Mayday! Mayday!*
his thumb was transmitting. Now he was
a hero; now he was an apostate;
now he wanted to go home. *What planet*
is this? Ignoring the Feds, he installed
a dreamcatcher and awaited the fallout.

As if suspended midair, the future
pilot crossed from one borough to the next,
navigating the subway on just
two buffalo. He could calculate;
he could climb. Seeing no tracks, he reached
clouds, stars, wind. Infinity (the number eight
propped on its side) beckoned. He was
without fear, alone, and seven years old.

TRUFFE DE CHINE

In my mother's kitchen, not one of us
ever dared to mention that unmistakable
odor. Clouds of it rose above our flat
noses, unspeakable, reminding us of
just where we came from. Predictable
phases of the moon served as excuses
to run out back for air. Stars dripped
brand-new dimes for us to spirit
away to Woolworth's. Our shoebox
shrine held ceramic deities to ward off
the endless dust of the highway
as well as typical domestic grease.

Meanwhile, clear across town, fungus
was used by our illustrious relations
to fete the likes of bandleaders and
chantoosies. According to our patriarch,
these were, of course, all basically
trash, but absolutely swell for
business: perpetually posing, crisscross
chopsticks midair, for gossip column
shutterbugs. Once past the Foo dogs
at the entrance, suburban bourgeoisie
squealed and let their tongues hang out
at the House of Exquisite Taste.

Arpège by Lanvin. Chanel Nos. 5 and 19.
I always knew where I was headed. What
I was headed for. Vetiver. Bulgarian rose.
Ambergris. When I inhaled the dust of
the endless highway, I exhaled to forget
how to want. Here at the bourse, a Chinese
truffle fetches a fraction of what a Périgord
will drag down. But the texture and taste
are compared to rubber. Earth. Mystery. Sweat.
Magic. Sex. Undercutting the competition. Infiltrating.
T. indicum is gaining ground, and somewhere,
a goddess encased in cardboard is smiling.

WHAT WE GIVE UP

I found Baby Jesus and took him
for my own, all his sweet plastic
pinkness just an inch or so
from praline so rich, it could kill.

When we kiss somebody new,
we imagine a savior
and start painting the picture we want.

Men I dated used to complain
I dressed like a nun. But that never
stopped them from trying
to undress me.

Day by day, I learn to let go.
Crossing a bridge alone, I discover
a garland of purple beads
and leave Baby Jesus right there.

I take it into my head
to deliver food to a soup kitchen
via mass transit; underground,
in unbleached linen, I am too shy
to ask, *Are you hungry?*

It hits me: If I continue fasting,
I may come to resemble
the stone wolf in my garden
with no memory of
the taste of human flesh.

I give up sound; I give up light.
I give up behavior that seemed
bred-in-the-bone, hard-core.
Items that used to cling
to my wrists and ankles
now huddle in boxes and bags,
ready for almsgiving.

Day number 40, I unzip my chest;
the process is messy but necessary.
I chew the tough, dry thought left over
from wishing. Then, leaving my heart
out on the curb, I nod
in the affirmative. It still hurts.

WHEN OUR PASSPORTS ARE INSPECTED

for the hundredth time, our government faces,
looking sharper than we do, fail to convince.
Staying in the moment, we improvise.

I'm recuperating from lifesaving surgery,
or, *When that was taken, I was in makeup*
and costume for a show. In the movie version

of this moment, we're haggling
at a souk (for a rug too beautiful
to abandon, too heavy to hold,
too obvious not to declare at customs)
and on the lookout for anyone

not our kind. (People ask how a peasant
could become a spy. The media all report
boilerplate backstory: not enough love
when she was a kid. Now she sees herself as
a saint performing the miracles, de rigueur,
one by one, reciting the lines you hear

in your own head. *No ordinary tourist*
in this country, I infiltrate the land of death.
Freedom will triumph in the end.) In real time,

you're lying in an expanse of white
demanding, *Untie my hands,* a credible
guerrilla in this intensive care unit,
so I can touch your face. One leg has already
started to turn black. But in the movie version

of this moment, you're in armor, yes, and
up the eastern side of the Eiffel Tower
from restless night to priceless sun.

WINGLESS

Pretty soon, I'm going
to hitch my back to a star
so that I can learn to fly.

Sure, in these modern times,
everybody and his dog
knows it's done with wires. But
what the hell. Wire me up.
Gird me in the harness.
I've been through worse.
Just let me believe the way I used to.

The body as seesaw: I see it now.
It's all in the hips: the point of balance.
When the body is lifted there,
it can maneuver like nobody's business.
It can even somersault. It can surely dance.
With the help of pulleys and counterweights,
the body can defy gravity.

I can see it, but I still can't do it.
Balance. Teach me that lesson
first. Now. Before anything else,
because nothing else is possible
without it. I'm either top-heavy
or I just don't function below the waist.

This is a body painfully aware
of its limits. The muscle spasms.
The growing pains. But
even worse than that, sometimes I fear

it's all in my head.

YES-HEART-GOODBYE

But it's late again already;
I'll have to tell it another time.

"Everything back in my mansion may be
broken," whispers a male of the species.
A fedora perches on his head while acid
burns his stomach. His aftershave is
an insistence of musk and sandalwood.
(Earlier in the day, he banished the rubble
and stench of a collapsed bathroom ceiling.)
As for this particular female, for the past
few weeks, she has slept on her left side
to wear out the heart a little faster.
Yet now she is leaning in closer to listen
for the rest of his lines. "Still, the chambers
I offer remain whole and full, and
the bounty of my arms is everlasting."
The seams of her fuchsia dress strain
to hold her in, but no matter. The legs
of these dancers have been backstitching,
cross-stitching, whipstitching. *Thighs, knees,*
anything you please. In the closed embrace,
not a dime would fit between their chests.
In the open embrace, the gravitational pull
is still obvious. *Elbows, arms, all that*
charms and disarms. And in the darkness, be it of
Fair Winds bordellos or of kitsch-glitz dancehalls
squeezed into disparaged outer boroughs
where airports or cemeteries can be found,
who cares if anyone can even remember
how to tell the truth. For this is the body:
a fortress as well as a vessel; a temple as well as a shell.

Born in Jersey City, New Jersey, **Judith Mary Gee** resided for many years in Chelsea, Manhattan, before finding her home in Park Slope, Brooklyn. It seems everywhere she lands becomes gentrified beyond recognition. She remains fascinated by that high/low dichotomy in status.

Gee holds a bachelor's degree in liberal arts from Sarah Lawrence College, where she studied writing with Cynthia Macdonald (two years, and Gee was Macdonald's teaching assistant), Jane Cooper, and Jean Valentine. Gee found them very different from Elizabeth Barrett Browning and Emily Dickinson, the female poets she knew from her childhood. Gee had long been disturbed by the widely accepted images of Barrett Browning and Dickinson: Fragile. Secluded. In aspic.

One of the college's special events was an appearance by Tillie Olsen. Gee felt Olsen's career had been ambushed by family responsibilities, and she was determined not to become a victim of that crime.

The hardest lesson Gee has had to learn is that she cannot control everything.

This poet has earned her living mainly as a copy editor at publishing houses and as a figure model at art schools.

In terms of career, Gee's relative Kim Chan has been her main role model. Popular success as an actor did not arrive until Chan was past conventional retirement age.

Following a prolonged hiatus of caregiving and breadwinning, Judith Mary Gee resumed the task of submitting poems for publication. This chapbook's acceptance was unexpected. Sheltering in place, locked down, isolated, watching the same cat video over and over, Gee initially failed to comprehend the message. Then at once, she straightened her back. The poet got up and danced.

www.ingramcontent.com/pod-product-compliance
Lightning Source LLC
LaVergne TN
LVHW051022080826
845145LV00009B/2754

* 9 7 8 1 6 4 6 6 2 3 9 5 2 *